# CLEAR
# COMMUNICATION

# POCKET EDITION

Published from
Mardukite Borsippa HQ, San Luis Valley, Colorado
Mardukite Academy & Systemology Society
*for spiritual or educational purposes only*

# CLEAR
# COMMUNICATION

## Systemology
## Professional Course
## Booklet #3

Developed by Joshua Free
for the Systemology Society

© 2023, JOSHUA FREE

ISBN : 978-1-961509-27-6

Pocket Paperback Edition — *November 2023*

**mardukite.com**

## Learn How To Let Your Spirit Fly...
## Then Chart Your Flight For Ascension!

Unlock your ultimate spiritual potential by removing barriers to your true native state.

Learn how to easily attain Self-actualization and help to actualize others along the way.

A greater appreciation and understanding of *Spiritual Life* and *Existence* awaits you. Expand your reach to achieve your dreams.

Each 'Professional Course' lesson-booklet offers simple exercises and techniques that directly apply the philosophy of Systemology, assisting to increase your true knowingness, improve your capabilities in this life, and even decide what you will do in your next.

At the Mardukite Academy of Systemology, the 'Professional Course' lessons in this series are presented to Seeker's that have completed the 'Basic Course', previously released as six lesson-booklets, or the six-in-one single volume edition "Fundamentals of Systemology."

This all new presentation of the Systemology 'Pathway-to-Ascension' takes Seekers and continuing students from "Zero" to "Infinity" at lightning-fast speeds!

## Discover Who You Really Are...
## Because You Were Never Human

# TABLET OF CONTENTS

# PROFESSIONAL
# COURSE
# INTRODUCTION

## WELCOME, SEEKER!
## LET'S CHART YOUR JOURNEY
## ON THE PATHWAY

*Systemology* is a "holistic" approach to understanding the human experience. It is not actually a singular "subject" in itself, but rather, a new way in which to view the many subjects of *Life* and all *Existence*.

This is a professional course in *Systemology*—specifically, how to *apply* the spiritual philosophy of *Mardukite Systemology* as a personal "*Pathway*" to Ascension. Our *Systemology* is a new approach to "*Self-Actualization*." It is completely relevant for the modern age and the future; and quite different from any previous similar attempts, or other traditions, you might find. What's more: it is applicable to anyone with any background.

This *"Professional Course"* series of lessons (booklets) immediately follows the material given in the *"Basic Course"* series—available as six separate pocket-sized booklets, or in a single hardcover volume titled: *"Fundamentals of Systemology: A New Thought For The 21st Century."*

This is a *new* presentation of *Systemology*, emphasizing the application of our philosophy for those *Seekers* that are *"Flying-Solo"*—or else working through their studies and exercises as solitary practitioners. This is a new innovation for *Systemology*. Aside from the book *"Crystal Clear,"* all of our former advanced courses have placed a focus on *"Traditional Piloting"*—where experienced practitioners assist *Seekers* in *"processing."*

To receive the greatest benefit from this study: it is expected that a *Seeker* will already be familiar with the fundamental concepts and terminology (previously relayed in the *Basic Course*) before using lessons from the *Professional Course*. This will allow us to cover the extensive territory of the *Pathway* much more quickly. However, for reference, a basic "*glossary*" of vocabulary used in this lesson is provided in the "*appendix*."

---

## A NEW VIEW OF THE HUMAN SPIRIT

*Systemology* is not a religion and does not require any type of *faith*. It is, however, built upon a "spiritual" premise—and as such is an "applied spiritual philosophy." It is based on ancient teachings that we are *Spiritual Beings* essentially "wearing" bodies like clothes—or using them as "vehicles." Yet our true native nature is not *physical*, but beyond this existence; and we can certainly operate a "body" from *outside* of it.

We are **all** *Spiritual Beings*—each of us a *unit* of *Spiritual Awareness*—that have experienced a very long *Spiritual Timeline* of existence. Although we might be particularly attached to the familiar "physical shells" associated with *this* lifetime, our true *"Spiritual Lifetime"* is seemingly *eternal*. We have been many things before *Human*, and we go onward as a *Spiritual Being* after our *"genetic vehicle"* of *this* incarnation perishes.

While a "spiritual" view of the *Human Condition* may not seem unique to our philosophy, just how often is the concept treated *systematically*? For that matter: just how many people, supposedly raised to this or that religion, or professing to believe one thing or another, actually live their lives as though they are *Spirits?*

As *Spiritual Beings* of immortal existence and infinite potential, we are not simply the *"creations"* of an even greater *Being-*

*ness*; we are, in fact, an integral part of that *"creative force"* which permeates all existence.

Our basic nature is to be a *"creative being"*—our highest goals are *"to create."* And as such a being—which we refer to as an *Alpha-Spirit* in *Systemology*—we have run into some difficulties along the course of our *Spiritual Timeline* and found ourselves trapped within material *Universes* of our own collaborative *creation*.

Since we did not start out our existence in a trapped condition, it is correct to say that we have *"fallen"* from our native *"godlike"* states. It did not happen all at one, but progressively and systematically. We know our "troubles" have resulted from accumulated "barriers" and "blockages"—or *fragmentation*—during our vast experiences as *Spiritual Beings*. They are not because we lack something; but because of what's been added.

In *Systemology*, we systematically examine those routes by which we must have descended to reach our present condition, then reverse the direction of travel and chart a personal "*Pathway to Ascension*." Of course, the exact "details" of the *Spiritual Timeline* will be different for each individual *Seeker*. However, we have been able to systematically chart our *Pathway* based on common patterns of *Human fragmentation*.

In the most basic terms: the *fragmentation* that defines our "downward spiral" consists of decisions or considerations where we deny our true nature. This includes those decisions to "*withdraw*" rather than "*reach*"; where we choose to *not-know* rather than *know*; to *not-communicate* rather than *communicate*; and ultimately, to take *no-responsibility* for being a *creative-cause*, and therefore succumb to being an *effect*.

But there is *hope!* And much more importantly: there is an effectively workable *way out* of the mazes and traps of our existence. If you are reading this now, you have already begun to gather your tools and build up the *"horsepower"* necessary to break the gravity holding your *Spiritual Beingness* to the *Human Condition*.

---

## STUDYING THE
## PROFESSIONAL COURSE

Most *Seekers* study and practice *Systemology* at-a-distance and independent of the "Mardukite Academy" or any "Master-level" mentors trained therein. This means that the *books* (and to a lesser degree, the *internet*) are the only means of direct contact a *Seeker* maintains with the "Systemology Society" during their studies. A continuing *Seeker* from the *"Basic Course"* will be familiar with the style of study found in *this* course.

Misunderstood words are the most common reason an individual abandons studying a subject. When a misunderstanding occurs, *Awareness* declines. These misunderstandings start to "stack up" after the first occurrence, and as a result, the level of interest and attention will also decline. This is how a "confusion" develops; and the individual will get "bored" with the subject, feel tired, and unable to concentrate.

One solution is to return to the part of the material that was still interesting and enjoyable to read. When scanning around that area of text, there is likely to be a new word (or new specific use of a familiar word) that is unclear, but was passed by unnoticed. All *Systemology* books include their own *glossary*. Using this *glossary* and a high-quality dictionary will help resolve this misunderstanding once it is located.

An effective education of any subject is taught on a *gradient*. This is what is intended by presenting the study of something as "*grades*." Rather than treating a subject as one total mass, true learning is achieved by increasing one's understanding with a *gradual* increase upward. The *ascent* to a mountaintop is not successfully achieved in one leap, but by targeting and reaching specific checkpoints along the way.

This *Professional Course* consists of a series of lessons (booklets) that gradually increase a *Seeker's* ability to understand and apply the practices and techniques of *Systemology* as a complete "*Pathway to Ascension*." It is an appropriate study for continuing *Seekers* (from the *Basic Course*), but also "advanced" *Systemologists*.

Each lesson (booklet) of the *Professional Course* applies *Systemology* to a particular subject (or focus). It is best if the entire course can be studied and applied in sequential order. These lessons also employ a style of practice or technique called "*Systematic Processing.*" An introduction to applying this methodology is provided in the final lesson (booklet) of the *Basic Course*—or in the "*Fundamentals of Systemology*" volume.

To study the *Professional Course* just like a student at the Academy: a *Seeker* reads through all instructional material and applies each exercise (or "*process*") presented in the text to the extent they comfortably can, before continuing on to the next lesson (booklet).

When first starting on the *Pathway* as a *Solo* practitioner, without the aid of an experienced *Pilot*, a *Seeker* shouldn't "push too hard" or allow themselves to get too "stuck" on any one area (lesson) or *process*. It is not expected that any one area will be completely handled when first introduced. For optimum results, it is expected that a serious *Seeker* will make more than one "pass" through the entire *Professional Course*.

The *Professional Course* is not altogether different from other forms of practical or technical education: where the instruction and exercises are delivered to a completion, and then a student further increases their abilities, strength and skill-level by applying additional practice throughout their life. Therefore, a student should not concern themselves with perfectly mastering each step (or lesson) before progressing forward.

Additional passes through the material are likely to result in different "*realizations*" (an increased *level of understanding*) than a previous time. New "layers" of *Knowingness* may now be accessible during a *process* that may not have been before. It is important to avoid invalidating the progress you've made just because one area is not completely handled right away, or if a certain *process* seems too difficult on the first pass.

---

## CHARTING A COURSE ON THE PATHWAY

Although we can communicate a systematic structure to *fragmentation,* the personal journey experienced along the *Pathway* will be different for each *Seeker.* For example, certain areas will seem more *"turbulent"* or difficult for one *Seeker* than another. We tend to say that these areas have more *"charge"* on them—or that they are more *"heavily charged."* It is best to handle such areas when you are already feeling "good" and not in a situation (or condition) where that specific area is consistently being *"triggered"* or *"restimulated."*

As an applied philosophy, *Systemology* "theory" can be easily utilized in the "laboratory" of the "world-at-large" in everyday life. This is implied within the basic instruction of each lesson. Unlike other "sciences" that conduct experiments by making a change to some "objective variable" *out there* and waiting to see an effect, our focus is the individual (or *Observer*) themselves, and how *they* affect the "*Reality*" perceived.

In addition to applying *Systemology* "New Thought" to everyday life, our philosophy is applied by using specific exercises and systematic techniques. These "*processes*" provide the most stable personal gain (and *realizations*) for each area; but only when actually applied with a *Seeker's* full "*presence*" and *Awareness*.

This *Professional Course* is designed so that it may be easily read and studied with little concern for what "dangers" these teachings—or *processing*—might unleash. However, there are still some guidelines that pertain to the "best-uses" of these course lessons, particularly if a *Seeker* intends for stable development.

Skipping over too much material/*processing* in early lessons may make attempts to understand (or apply) later lessons more difficult. However, once the complete *Professional Course* is worked through at least once in its entirety, specific areas can then be later returned to and treated with a greater sense of *Awareness* and *"presence"* than before. Of course, in *"Traditional Piloting,"* the rate of processing is monitored by an experienced practitioner; but in *"Solo-Processing,"* a *Seeker* must regulate their own progress on the *Pathway*.

Applying a systematic technique is called *"running a process."* The *processes* are designed with very simple instructions or "*command-lines*." To *run* a *processing command-line*, a *Seeker* may be assisted by the communication of that *line* from a "*Co-Pilot*" (as in "*Traditional Piloting*"). But even then, a *Seeker* must still personally "input" the *command* as *Self*. For this reason —and quite thankfully— *Solo-Processing* is possible.

## TAKING FLIGHT ON THE PATHWAY

*Processing Techniques* are intended to treat the *Spiritual Being* or *Alpha-Spirit*; the individual themselves. It is applied by the *Alpha-Spirit*—then *Self-directed* to the "Mind-System" or even a "body" (*genetic-vehicle*), both of which are "constructs" that the *Alpha-Spirit* (*Self*, or the "I-AM" *Awareness* unit) operates, but neither of which is actually *Self*. *Fragmentation* causes *Humans* to falsely identify *Self* as the "*Mind*" or even a "*Body*."

The *Professional Course* lessons (booklets) are designed for the *Beginning Seeker* in mind—one that may have an understanding of theory, but with little experience in practice. That being said: each of these lessons may be used toward total *Beta-Defragmentation* within a specific area. There are also more *processes* given for each subject than may be necessary to achieve an *ultimate end-point realization* on that entire area.

Some *processes* can be treated quite lightly at first; others may require a bit of working at in order to get *"running"* well. It is important to set aside a period of time when you can be dedicated to your studies and *processing*. This period of time is referred to as a *"processing session."* The reason for this, is that when a *process* does start *running* well, it is important to be able to complete it to a satisfactory *"end-point."*

The purpose of *systematic processing* is to be able to *really* "look" at things and even determine the *considerations* we have made—or attitudes we have decided—about *Reality* as a result of those experiences. It doesn't do us much good to simply "glance"—or to *restimulate* something uncomfortable and then quickly *withdraw* from it once again, leaving more of our *attention* yet again behind and held fixedly on it.

Generally speaking, a *Seeker* continues to *run* a *process* so long as something is "happening"—which is to say, the *process* is still producing a change. Usually this is evident by the type of "answers" that a *command-line* helps a *Seeker* originate from the database of their own *Mind-System*. The *command-lines* do not "do" anything on their own. They assist a *Seeker* to direct their own attention toward increasing *Awareness*.

Of course, a *Seeker* may also cease to generate new "data" from a *process* without reaching an *"ultimate"* realization as an *"end-point."* It is possible that additional "layers" (or even other "areas") require handling before anything "deeper" is accessible. If this is the case, end the *process*. But, if a *Seeker* is *withdrawing* from something uncomfortable that was incited or stirred up, then a *process* is *run* until they feel "good" about it.

In case the thought of encountering *"turbulence"* is a concern: the techniques given as *"Opening Procedures"* of a *Formal Session* (in the *Basic Course*), and those found in the earliest lessons of the *Professional Course*, are quite useful when applied as "safety nets" for maintaining *Awareness* and *presence*, even when *Flying-Solo*.

One of the benefits to *Flying-Solo* is that *processing* is entirely *Self-determined*. This already provides a certain built-in "safety" for a practitioner. Anything you *restimulate* by *Self-determinism* is *your thing*. It is not incited by external *other-determined* influences (or other "sourcepoints" in existence) that make you an *effect*. It can be more easily handled in *processing*—or you can simply let things "cool down" and come back to it again.

While it may seem "mysterious" to beginners, a *Seeker* gets a sense for knowing how long to *run* a *process* only with practice. Once you have spent some time actually applying the *Professional Course*, there are many aspects that become "second nature" because they are, in fact, a part of our true original nature. All we have done is *"reverse engineer"* the routes of *creation* and *consideration* that are already *our own*.

# LESSON THREE: CLEAR COMMUNICATION

---
### NEW SYSTEMATIC PROCESSES
### INTRODUCED IN THIS LESSON

- Expanding Willingness (*subjective proc.*)
  [*"Willing To"*]
- Communication Processing (*"circuits"*)
- Communication Processes (*objective vers.*)
  [*"Hello!"*]
- Acknowledgment (*objective processes*)
- Willingness To Duplicate (*subjective*)
- *"Bell, Book & Candle"*

---
### EXISTING APPLICATIONS
### DISCUSSED IN THIS LESSON

- Beta-Awareness (*Basic Course*)
- Formal Session (*Basic Course*)
- Control of Mind-Body (*Lesson #1*)
- Subjective Processing (*Lesson #2*)

## WILLINGNESS TO REACH FURTHER

Stable progress on the *Pathway-to-Ascension* is marked by states of increased "*Knowingness*." By this, we mean what a person *actually knows*. This *Knowingness* is quite different from what we are *told*, or other *associative knowledge*. We mean specifically: what a person already *knows* about *Self*, their *past*, *Life*, and all *Existence* —but, for whatever reasons, has "*blocked out*" from their present *Awareness*.

The long-run of the *Pathway-to-Ascension* is intended to return to an individual the *certainty* and *Knowingness* of their original native "*god-like*" state as an immortal *Alpha-Spirit*. We do not expect this to happen all at once; and there are many safeguards of the Mind-System that prevent the flood-gates of total *Knowingness* from overwhelmingly "*caving-in*" on the *Seeker* all at once.

*Spiritual fragmentation* (which also includes matters of emotion and thought) accumulates beneath the surface of what an individual is presently *aware* of. Some use the words "unconscious" or "subconscious"—but these are not truly *systematic* terms. Yet, we do mean what is happening *unknowingly*.

In *Lesson #2* of this *Professional Course* series, we introduced the idea of a continuous "*Spiritual Timeline,*" a "memory" that the individual carries of their eternal existence as an *Alpha-Spirit*. This includes the experience of *this* incarnation or "lifetime" as well as all others.

Having the entire memory of one's past—or *Backtrack*—"*resurface*" on them in one flash instant would be too overwhelming to behold. But it can safely occur gradually—and *Systematic Processing* is intended to help gradually restore *Knowingness* of the full basic state or *identity* of the individual as a *Spiritual Being*.

Of course, to accomplish these goals, one of the first requirements is that a *Seeker* actually be *"Willing to Know."*

In the previous *"Fundamentals of Systemology"* *Basic Course* series, we described the totality of *Awareness* as a "spectrum" divided into two main areas: what is clearly *known* and a dark area that is *not-known*. The dividing line between forms the basis for what is considered *"above"* or *"below"* the *"surface"* of *thought*.

This "line" is really a philosophical construct; so we aren't trying to move the "line." In *processing*, however, we are working to shift more of the *data* from the area of *"not-known"* to the area of *"known."* There is also a "gray area" of what is *almost-known*; what is *accessible* to a *Seeker* but remains *just* "beneath the surface."

The greater the *Willingness-to-Know,* and the more that is within an individual's *tolerance* to reach for, the "wider" or "larger" this *gray area* will be for what is *accessible* in *processing*. *Systematic Processing* both *accesses* what is *accessible* and increases the individual's *tolerance* to *confront* addition layers beneath it.

*Fragmentation* is handled as a series of layers—each layer representing a level of blockage. We don't usually make stable gains by simply digging a deep hole to what is buried far beneath. Too much of what surrounds at each layer will "cave-in" on the *Seeker*. Therefore, we strip away the debris in layers to expose the entire area underneath.

We have introduced the fundamentals of *systematic processing*—specifically *subjective-universe processing*—in the previous lessons of this *Professional Course*. Included with this is advice and tips for handling *processes* as a *Solo-Pilot*, and a few maneuvers for getting yourself out of trouble if you encounter turbulence. With that in mind, let's start this lesson off with some light *processing*.

[Note: if you have already attained the ultimate *realizations* as *end-points* for any particular area (from a previous pass through this course material), then your practical instruction is to "*spot*" the moment it happened.]

## EXPANDING WILLINGNESS

For *processes* like these, you want to *run* through as many cycles of the "*processing command-lines*" ("PCL") as you can, rather than dwelling on each individual answer. You want to generate a response as if it were an item on a list, then go to the next, rather than free-wheeling into an entire narrative or explanation.

Each *process* that follows here will consist of three PCL. These are *run* repetitively as an alternating cycle (1, 2, 3, 1, 2, 3...) until you feel good about doing the *process* (which is the *end-point* of the process).

The ultimate goal is to genuinely increase one's *Willingness-to-Reach* in whatever area is being treated, since ultimately a *"god-like"* being would be *willing* to *know, do, communicate* or *experience* anything, whether or not they actually choose to. There is another aspect to these *processes* that increases *willingness* to "grant" or "permit" others their own *"Beingness"* — to also allow others the freedom to *Be*.

Willingness To Find Out

1. *"What would you be willing to find out about yourself?"*
2. *"What would you be willing to find out about someone else?"*
3. *"What would you be willing for someone else to find out?"*

In this *process*, the phrase *"find out"* could be substituted with *"know."* And *"would you be*" is a basic, less intrusive, wording that is often used with beginning *Seekers*; but a more direct PCL approach is "*are you.*" We will apply the direct approach here:

Willingness To Have

1. "*What are you willing to have?*"
2. "*What are you willing for someone else to have?*"
3. "*What are you willing for others to have?*"

In this instance, "*someone else*" means a specific person (*terminal*); whereas "*others*" is meant to include everyone in a particular group, for example: all other "*Humans.*" Let's do some more of this *processing.*

Willingness To Do

1. "*What are you willing to do?*"
2. "*What are you willing for someone else to do?*"
3. "*What are you willing for others to do?*"

Willingness To Be

1. *"What are you willing to be?"*

2. *"What are you willing for someone else to be?"*

3. *"What are you willing for others to be?"*

When we speak of *willingness* and *accessibility,* we tend to also use the word *"tolerance."* This means what is within an individual's *willingness* to *confront.* One of the areas that a *Seeker* may actually *process* for greater *tolerance* in general regards "change." The most basic *process* is to *alternate* the following PCL repeatedly.

A. *"What would you be willing to have change?"*

B. *"What would you be willing to have remain the same?"*

An *objective* example of this same *process* is:

*"Look around the room; Spot some things you would be willing to have change?"*

*"Spot some things you would be willing to
remain the same?"*

One of the reasons that so much of our
existence remains in the realm of "not-
known" is because of our avoidance of
actually *confronting* the contents of "what
lies beneath." In many cases, there is a
deeply laden *fear* that inhibits our *Willingness-to-Know*. Or a person stops *"look-
ing"* and starts "thinking" and worrying
from a point of confusion instead.

*Knowingness* is preferred to *thinking*.
There's nothing inherently wrong with
*thinking*, except that it usually originates
from a *fragmented* state and is used to
substitute actual *Knowingness*. The worst
fears generally concern what is *"not-
known"* (or "unknown"), and not what an
individual actually understands or
*knows*. So, let's just get some of that out in
the open with this next *process*, before we
continue.

*"Think of, or imagine, a horrible 'truth' that you might find out."*

*"What would be the consequence of that?"*

---

## SYSTEMOLOGY & COMMUNICATION

Communication is a central subject to *Systemology*, because we consider *all interactions* between "systems" to be a "communication." In fact, "*Systematic Processing*" is entirely based on our understanding of communication from within the philosophy of *Systemology*. And in many ways, we are really treating various aspects of communication consistently all along the *Pathway*.

In *Systemology*, "communication" is *systematically* handled as a *flow*. This allows us to treat all types of communication; not simply the "speech" and "gestures" we quickly associate with it, in terms of the *Human* experience. *Flows* occur on a "*channel*" between two *terminals* — usually *you* and something else.

A *Seeker* may notice similarities between our *Systemology of Communication* and the way in which "*water motion*" or "*electricity*" is understood in other applications. Either of these could be used to demonstrate our principles. We will focus on "water" for the moment, rather than assume an understanding of *electricity*.

Running water is a type of *communication*. Although we treat it all inclusively as a "body" of water, it is actually composed of individual droplets, each of which might be thought of as a single "unit" of water. In a stream, the activity of *flow-motion* represents the communication. It allows a single "unit" to cross a *distance*, from a source-point to a destination-point within a certain period of *time*. Therefore, *motion* and *time* are connected.

*Fragmentation* is that which "blocks" *free-flow* on a *channel*. It creates a "dam" for an otherwise fluid current. And as we know, concerning water blockages and dams, this has a tendency to build up "pressure." In our *processing*, this "pressure" is equivalent to the *"charge"* or *"turbulence"* that is encountered for a given area.

Inhibited communication, and control of these *flows* by outside (*other-determined*) sources, is what leads to our greatest upsets in life; it leads to violent protests, compulsions, reactivity, automation, and other societal misfortune.

Fortunately, control over these *"communication barriers"* ultimately remains our own. For, regardless of the reasons, it is ourselves (as an *Alpha-Spirit*) that decides to go "out-of-communication" with a *terminal*, or to relinquish *knowing* control over the *flow* on a particular *channel*.

With enough *actualized* or focused *attention*, you can systematically push through any personal *communication barrier* without even having to address all the reasons for its being there. In the case of "basic" *Human* communication, most barriers are crossed simply by *quantity* and *volume*.

For example: if you were to talk enough about a particular area, you would eventually find yourself uninhibited about communicating that subject. The reverse of this, or how we become inhibited, is when an "outside" (*other-determined*) source repeatedly demands (or even enforces with actions) that we *stop* that *flow* of communication each time we *start* it.

*Systematic Processing* resolves this by encouraging a *flow* until the barriers are cleared away. This is one of the benefits to *Traditional Piloting* for some *processes*; because another individual is there to keep those cycles of communication *flow-*

*ing* along a *channel,* without the *Seeker* feeling the need to *"hold back."*

Outside of our philosophy, a more familiar *"New Thought"* technique involves a practice of writing letters to individuals that we have difficulties communicating with—or about certain subjects. We don't actually send these letters, but it gets us to externalize a flow (out on paper) that is otherwise being held in. There is no pressure to actually engage in communication with the other person until we feel comfortable doing so.

If we were to extend this practice *systematically,* we would also include writing letters from the perspective (or *point-of-view*) of the *other* person, as if they are writing *to* us. This allows us to handle both the *"out-flow"* and the *"in-flow"* on a *channel,* between us and a *terminal.*

In *Systemology,* we also refer to these various *flow*-types as the *"circuits"* of a *chan-*

*nel*. These circuits are usually numbered: 1, 2 and 3. They correspond with the numbers given to the three PCL in many *processes*. They concern:

1, *out-flow*, what we project or send;

2, *in-flow*, what we receive; and

3, *cross-flow*, what we perceive or observe of others.

Communication is experienced on these three *circuits* of a *channel*; and on these same *circuits* we store our *fragmented data*. Let us see this directly in an example of *"communication processing."*

1. *"What would you be willing to say to someone?"*

2. *"What would you be willing to have someone say to you?"*

3. *"What would you be willing to have someone say to others?"*

The PCL are *run* in rotation. The procedural instruction is to *"spot"* specific things that you are willing to communicate about. It is possible that there are many specific areas that require additional *processing* later in order to handle completely, so be sure not to invalidate the progress and gains that you actually do make along the way by feeling like you are still "avoiding" certain things.

This *process* is *run* until you feel an increased freedom in ability to communicate. The ultimate *end-point* on this would be total uninhibited communication about anything—regardless of what you actually choose to, or not to, communicate about.

An advanced upper-level application of this same *process* is included for consideration.

1. *"What would you be willing to 'read' in someone's mind?"*

2. *"What would you be willing to have someone 'read' in your mind?"*

3. *"What would you be willing to have
   someone 'read' in another's mind?"*

---

## COMMUNICATION PROCESSES

The subject of *communication* is handled
in various areas throughout the entire
*Pathway.* Elsewhere, in more advanced
material, we also treat movement of a
*"particle"* as communication. For now, let
us focus on what is most familiar for the
*Human Condition;* mainly, observable
communications that originate from a
*lifeform.*

What is considered *magic* or *mysticism* is
simply a handling of *communication* originating from an *Alpha* "spiritual" existence. This includes our own *"Alpha
Thought"* or *"postulates"* as a *Spiritual Being* (separate and superior to a construc-
ted *"Mind-System."* A *postulate* is a
"decision for things "to be" or "not be." It

does not originate from a "brain" or any-where within *this* Physical Universe; it *impinges* on, or *perturbs* activity in, this Universe via a *communication* of *intention*.

*Communication* is a broadcast, projection or *out-flow* of something from one point to another, across some distance. In *Human communication*, the "words" and method of delivery are secondary factors to the actual *intention* itself. Before any words are chosen, or any visible activity occurs, an *intention* is made. There is also an intended *receipt-point* or "destination" for the *communication* to "arrive" at.

For example: when these *Professional Course* lessons are developed, there is an intended "message" and an intended "audience" for it. The choice of words and arrangement into booklets then follows thereafter. A *true communication* cycle only occurs when its "meaning" is *duplicated* at the receipt-point exactly as intended. *Professional Pilots* must be expertly trained and skilled in this area to deliver *processing* to others.

Where *communication* concerns the individual or *Seeker*, we are most concerned with *intention*—the increase of strength and clarity of *intention*. With enough *intention* behind the meaning, you might even say the wrong words and others will still be able to *duplicate* the understanding implied. There are all various kinds of phenomenon in the area of *communication* that we will practice here.

*"Choose an object."*

*"Say 'Hello' to it repeatedly."*

*"Notice the point in space you are projecting each 'Hello'."*

*"Directly intend them to various specific points surrounding (or next to) the object."*

*"Now intently focus them right into the center of the object."*

This is practiced with different objects until a *Seeker* feels they have a handle on projecting *intention* into specific points. Once this is practiced with a deliberate concentration of focus, a *Seeker* then performs the action more rapidly with various objects throughout the room, and *intending* to land the "*Hello*" in the direct center of each without having to strain (or lingering for more than a moment on one point).

"*Invent a nonsense word and intend for it to mean 'Hello'.*"

Practice the previous exercises, but speak the "nonsense word" as you intend your *communication*. Then practice this with other random words that you intend to mean "*Hello.*" The *end-point* on this is a greater sense that *meaning* and *intention* is separate from the words and sounds *communicated* from the "*Body.*"

Practice projecting *intention* with force as you shout "*Hello!*" at the objects. Alternate this with "whispering" it; but the emphasis here should be on sensing the same strong *intention* regardless of volume.

Finally, practice intending your *"Hello"* silently. This doesn't mean just sitting there and "thinking" the word. Get the same sense of *intention* as when you were using words and sound to *communicate* it. Alternate this with speaking the word, until you can maintain the strength of the *intention* when silent.

"One-way" *flows* of communication can sometimes feel depleting if *run* too long in the same direction. You may have noticed that during a publicity event or workshop that the "Q-and-A's" or more personal "book-signing" segments take place *after* an individual lectures or reads. This allows a natural *replenishing* of *attention units* that have otherwise been directed or projected *outward* for a long period of time.

You can actually balance this out in the above *processing* exercises by *imagining* that the objects are saying *"Hello"* to you, placing you at the *receipt-point*. The emphasis here should be on also spotting the object as a *source-point* of the *communication*. [At no time do we expect the object to audibly say *"Hello."*]

---

## ACKNOWLEDGMENT PROCESSES

In two-way *communication*, there is another component to a true cycle: *acknowledgment*. The message crosses a distance from a *source-point* to a *receipt-point*, and the "receiver" *acknowledges* that the message has been received. This completes a full cycle-of-action. Another cycle may then begin.

Compulsive attempts to *communicate* result from lack of *acknowledgment*. An individual continues to *outflow* until they can sense that their intention has been received. You may have observed this in everyday life, where an individual continues to basically say the same thing until the receiver finally says, *"okay, I get it."*

In *Traditional Piloting*, acknowledgment is essential for completing a cycle or PCL. A *Pilot* directs the PCL; the *Seeker* receives it and performs the action; the *Pilot* completes the cycle with an *acknowledgment* — usually "okay," "thank you," "all right," *&tc*. This is a critical part of *systematic processing* when it is "Co-Piloted." In *Solo-Piloting*, a *Seeker* still acknowledges to themselves (e.g. *"okay"*) when an action (or PCL) is completed.

An acknowledgment is also a communication — and therefore carries its own *intention*. In the everyday life example above, a person might intend their acknowledgment to mean either, *"okay, I see what you're saying"* or *"okay, I heard you a hundred times already, just shut up."*

Using the previous *"communication processes"* as a model of practice, let us do some exercises that concern the area of acknowledgment.

*"Imagine objects in the room saying 'Hello' to you."*

*"Acknowledge each 'Hello' by saying 'Thank You' out loud."*

As before, a *Seeker* can also practice this by intending a "silent" acknowledgment, once they have a sense for it with words and sound. And, as before, a sense of the actual *intention* is the emphasis of the *process*.

---

## DUPLICATION AND REPRODUCTION

There are two main aspects of *duplication* that directly affect a *Seeker*—in *processing* or otherwise: the ability to duplicate an action (the same thing repeatedly); and the ability to copy the meaning of what is being communicated, or to even put an advanced spin on it, to duplicate someone else's *"point-of-view"* ("POV").

Ability to properly handle duplication is critical to the "spiritual well-being" of the *Alpha-Spirit*. Having experienced a very long existence, an individual that has suffered from many undesirable incidents will likely go "out-of-communication" (or "out-of-reach") with such areas, finding it unacceptable that these things should repeat. This develops into automatic-reactivity that make us reluctant to repeat anything.

There is also the factor of *imprints* on the *Backtrack* remaining from lifetimes spent in slavery—often forced to do repetitive tasks under duress. There is a lot of *turbulence* in this area for most *Humans*, and it has caused an increase of unhappiness and illness when triggered or restimulated in modern society. Of course, if *"du-*

*plication*" is *processed*, a *Seeker* can experience a relief from the discomfort associated with it.

As has been the general method in these early lessons, we'll start with the "*Willingness*" to *duplicate*. This is a light *subjective process*.

1. "*What would you be willing to have happen again?*"
2. "*What would someone else be willing to have happen again?*"
3. "*What would others be willing to have happen again?*"

In this instance, it may be apparent that our systematic approach of revolving circuits is also meant to keep a *Seeker* from *running* a single *flow*-type for too long. Repetitive-style *processing* is sometimes *run* in *Co-Piloted* sessions, because ultimately we are mostly concerned with the first PCL. But for a *process* like this, a *Solo-Pilot* will assuredly not get the most significant results by continuously *running* that one *flow* alone.

---

## "BELL, BOOK & CANDLE"

The *"2020 Professional Piloting Course"*—now collected in the *"Metahuman Destinations"* volumes—occurred shortly after release of the first two advanced publications: *"The Tablets of Destiny Revelation"* and *"Crystal Clear: Handbook for Seekers."* During this time, we spent a lot of time experimenting with methods of increasing a *Seeker's "presence in-session."* The subject of *"duplication"* sprung up continuously.

In the original version used at the *Systemology Society*: a bell, a book, and a candle, are all placed on the table in front of the *Seeker.* They select two of the items and the third is put away. This validates a *Seeker's* power of choice at the start of the *process.* This may be performed with *any* two *dissimilar* objects.

A version of this now appears in our modern practice (script) of a *Formal Session*, in the "*Opening Procedures*" listed as "Control of Body and Mind In-Session." In those instructions: the items are placed within reach; or alternatively, at two points in the room (preferably on tables), in which a *command-line* for "walking between" would be inserted in the *process.* [Objects are listed as "*Item-1*" and "*Item-2.*"]

"*Pick up Item-1.*"

"*Notice its weight.*"

"*Notice its color.*"

"*Notice its texture.*"

"*Put it down.*"

"*Pick up Item-2.*"

"*Notice its weight.*"

"*Notice its color.*"

*"Notice its texture."*

*"Put it down."*

This is performed repeatedly over and over again; but it is not really as simple as it seems. Each cycle must be performed just as if it is the "first time" and *not* simply as an "automated repeat" action. One of our goals with this *process* is to *"run out"* — or *"process out"* — the reactive tendency of putting repetitive action "on automatic." It also treats the tendency of *re-creating* the *past* as the *present*.

To be extremely effective and provide stable results, it is not uncommon at first to *run* this *process* in excess of 20-30 minutes, and then for as long as an hour or two. This is not how it is treated as an *Opening Procedure* in a typical *Formal Session*; but, it may be when it is first introduced to a *Seeker* by a *Professional*. It is also not uncommon to experience the entire *"Beta-Awareness Scale"* of *emotional* and *mental* states while *running* this.

As a *Self-determined Alpha-Spirit*, there is nothing inherently wrong with setting a "system" or creating a "mechanism" to do things "on automatic" *knowingly* by choice. Unfortunately, there is a lot of this built into the *Human Condition* that is experienced *unknowingly*. Therein lies the *fragmenting* factor.

It is certainly within the capabilities of a *"god-like"* being to perform the same action repeatedly without giving in to any "hypnotic effect." Properly *running* "Bell, Book & Candle" allows a *Seeker* the practice of breaking "hypnotic effects" of repetition—but only when seeing each performance of the cycle as a "new action," intended in its own unit of time, and not the cumulative copy of the past.

There is an advanced application of this *process* that may be applied on additional passes through this material (if it is found to be above a *Seeker's* present skill level). A *Seeker* should be well practiced with the standard ("physical") version of this as given above—and *run* it for a few cycles in the same session before applying the advanced ("mental"-"eyes closed") version.

This practice works best if you are able to *imagine* or visualize a *"space,"* rather than simply *creating* the two objects in your mind. For example, you can image the corners of a cube or a room and then add the walls, floor and ceiling. Make this large enough that it extends above, below and behind the *viewpoint* (or "POV") that you are perceiving this imagery from. [There is *no* reason to imagine yourself as a *body* in that room.]

*"Create (or 'imagine') two tables in the room."*

*"Create 'Item-1' on one of them; and 'Item-2' on the other."*

*"Intend for 'Item-1' to float up above the table."*

*"Notice its weight; Notice its color; Notice its texture."*

*"Intend for it to float back down."*

*"Intend for 'Item-2' to float up above the table."*

*"Notice its weight; Notice its color; Notice its texture."*

*"Intend for it to float back down."*

Practice the steps in alternation, as with the standard ("physical") version.

- - - -

Working through the first, second, and third lessons (booklets) of the *Professional Course,* marks completion of "*Systemology Level-0.*" It demonstrates all of the skills necessary for a *Seeker* (or *Pilot*) to conduct a *Formal Session* and perform *systematic processing* for additional "levels" that remains on the *Pathway-to-Ascension.*

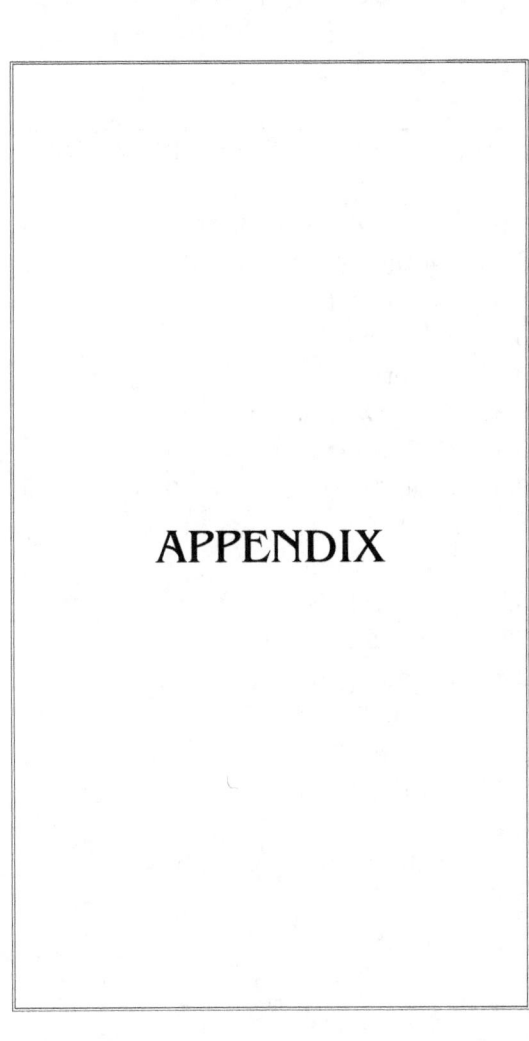

APPENDIX

# APPENDIX: BETA-AWARENESS SCALE

**4.0** SELF-HONESTY (BETA)
3.9 "Vibrant" ("Charismatic")
3.8 "Enthusiastic" ("In Love")
3.7 "Energetic"
3.6 "Cheerful"
**3.5** CONFIDENT ("Positive")
3.4 "Determined"
3.3 "Eager"
3.2 "Alert" ("Attentive")
3.1 "Strong Interest"
**3.0** INTERESTED ("Content")
2.9 "Small Interest"
2.8 "Encouraged"
2.7 "Disinterested"
2.6 "Doubtful"
**2.5** INDIFFERENT ("Tolerant")
2.4 "Bored"
2.3 "Dislike" ("Neglectful")
2.2 "Tired"
2.1 "Monotony"

**2.0**  INVALIDATING ("Pessimistic")

1.9  "Antagonism"

1.8  "Suffering" ("In Pain")

1.7  "Confrontational"

1.6  "Violent"

**1.5**  ANGRY ("Negative")

1.4  "Hateful"

1.3  "Spiteful"

1.2  "Resentment"

1.1  "Anxiety"

**1.0**  FEAR ("Afraid")

0.9  "Terror"

0.8  "Numb"

0.7  "Evasive"

0.6  "Loss"

**0.5**  GRIEF ("Sadness")

0.4  "Depression"

0.3  "Victimization"

0.2  "Hopelessness"

0.1  "Apathy" ("Unconsciousness")

**0.0**  BETA CONTINUITY (Organic Death)

# GLOSSARY

**actualization** : to make actual, not just potential; to bring into full solid Reality; to realize fully in *Awareness* as a "thing."

**agreement (reality)** : unanimity of opinion of what is "thought" to be known; an accepted arrangement of how things are; things we consider as "real" or as an "is" of "reality"; a consensus of what is real as made by standard-issue (common) participants; what an individual contributes to or accepts as "real"; in *Systemology*, a synonym for "*reality.*"

**alpha** : the first, primary, basic, superior or beginning of some form; in *Systemology*, referring to the state of existence operating on spiritual archetypes and postulates, will and intention "exterior" to the low-level condensation and solidarity of energy and matter as the 'physical universe' (*beta*).

**alpha-spirit** : a "spiritual" *Life*-form; the "true" *Self* or I-AM; the *individual*; the spiritual (*alpha*) *Self* that is animating the (*beta*) physical body or "*genetic vehicle*" using a continuous *Lifeline* of spiritual ("*ZU*") energy; an individual spiritual (*alpha*) entity possessing no physical mass or measurable waveform (motion) in the Physical Universe as itself, so it animates the (*beta*) physical body or "*genetic vehicle*" as a catalyst to experience *Self*-determined causality in effect within the *Physical Universe*; a singular unit or point of *Spiritual Awareness* that is *Aware* that it is *Aware*.

**alpha thought** : the highest spiritual *Self-determination* over creation and existence exercised by an Alpha-Spirit; the Alpha range of pure *Creative Ability* based on direct postulates and considerations of *Beingness*; spiritual qualities comparable to "thought" but originating in Alpha-existence, independently superior to a Mind-System.

**ascension** : actualized *Awareness* elevated to the point of true "spiritual existence" exterior to *beta existence*. An "Ascended Master" is one who has returned to an incarnation on Earth as an inherently *Enlightened One*, demonstrable in their words and actions; they have the ability to *Self-direct* the "Mind" and "Body" as *Self* (as a "Spirit"); and to maintain consciousness as a personal identity continuum with the same *Self-directed* control and communication of Will-Intention that is exercised, actualized and developed deliberately during one's present incarnation.

**associative knowledge** : significance or meaning of a facet or aspect assigned to (or considered to have) a direct relationship with another facet; to connect or relate ideas or facets of existence with one another; in traditional systems logic, an equivalency of significance or meaning between facets or sets that are grouped together, such as in *(a + b) + c = a + (b + c)*; in Systemology, erroneous associative knowledge is assignment of the same value to all facets or parts considered as related (even when they are not actually so), such as in *a = a, b = a, c = a* and so forth without distinction.

**attention** : active use of *Awareness* toward a specific aspect or thing; the act of "attending" with the presence of *Self*; a direction of focus or concentration of *Awareness* along a particular channel or conduit or toward a particular terminal node or communication termination point; the Self-directed concentration of personal energy as a combination of observation, thought-waves and consideration; focused application of *Self-Directed Awareness*.

**awareness** : the highest sense of-and-as *Self* in knowing and being as I-AM (the *Alpha-Spirit*); the extent of beingness directed as a viewpoint (POV) experienced by *Self* as knowingness.

**beta (existence)** : all manifestation in the "Physical Universe" (KI, in *Zuism*); the conditions of *Awareness* for the *Alpha-spirit* (*Self*) as a physical organic *Lifeform* or "*genetic vehicle*" in which it experiences causality in the *Physical Universe*.

**charge** : to fill or furnish with a quality; to supply with energy; to lay a command upon; in *Systemology*—to imbue with intention; to overspread with emotion; personal energy stores and significances entwined as fragmentation in mental images, reactive-response encoding and intellectual (and/or) programmed beliefs.

**circuit** : a circular path or loop; a closed-path within a system that allows a flow; a pattern or action or wave movement that follows a specific route or potential path only; in *Systemology*, "*communication processing*" pertaining to a specific *flow* of energy or information along a channel; "*feedback loop.*"

**communication** : successful transmission of information, data, energy (&tc.) along a message line, with a reception of feedback; an energetic flow of intention to cause an effect (or duplication) at a distance; the personal energy moved or acted upon by will or else 'selective directed attention'; the 'messenger action' used to transmit and receive energy across a medium; also relay of energy, a message or signal—or even locating a personal POV (viewpoint) for the Self—along the *ZU-line*.

**confront** : to come around in front of; to be in the presence of; to stand in front of, or in the face of; to meet "face-to-face" or "face-up-to"; additionally, in *Systemology*, to fully tolerate or acceptably withstand an encounter with a particular manifestation or encounter.

**defragmentation** : the *reparation* of wholeness; collecting all dispersed parts to reform an original whole; a process of removing "*fragmentation*" in data or knowledge to provide a clear understanding; applying techniques and processes that promote a *holistic* interconnected *alpha* state, favoring observational *Awareness* of continuity in all spiritual and physical systems; in *Systemology*, a "*Seeker*" achieving actualized "*Self-Honest Awareness*" is said to be in a basic state of *beta-defragmentation*, whereas *Alpha-defragmentation* is the rehabilitation of the *creative ability*, managing the *Spiritual Timeline* and the POV of *Self* as Alpha-Spirit (I-AM).

**fragmentation** : breaking into parts and scattering the pieces; the *fractioning* of wholeness or the *fracture* of a holistic interconnected *alpha* state, favoring observational *Awareness* of perceived connectivity between parts; *discontinuity*; separation of a totality into parts; in *Systemology*, a person outside of *Self-Honesty* is said to be operating from a *fragmented* state.

**flow** : movement across (or through) a channel (or conduit); a direction of active energetic motion, typically distinguished as either an *in-flow, out-flow* or *cross-flow.*

**genetic-vehicle** : a physical *Life*-form; the physical (*beta*) body that is animated/controlled by the (*Alpha*) *Spirit* using a continuous *Spiritual Lifeline* (ZU); a physical (*beta*) organic receptacle and catalyst for the (*Alpha*) *Self* to operate "causes" and experience "effects" within the *Physical Universe.*

**holistic** : the examination of interconnected systems as encompassing something greater than the *sum* of their "parts."

**Human Condition** : a standard default state of Human experience that is generally accepted to be the extent of its potential identity (*beingness*) —currently treated as *Homo Sapiens Sapiens,* but which is scheduled for replacement by *Homo Novus* (the "New Human").

**imprint** : to strongly impress, stamp, mark (or outline) onto a softer 'impressible' substance; to mark with pressure onto a surface; in *Systemology*, used to indicate permanent Reality impressions marked by frequencies, energies or interactions experienced during periods of emotional distress, pain, unconsciousness, loss, enforcement, or something antagonistic to physical (personal) survival, all of which are are stored with other reactive response-mechanisms at lower-levels of *Awareness* as opposed to the active memory database and proactive processing center of the Mind; an experiential "memory-set" that may later resurface—be triggered or stimulated artificially—as Reality, of which similar responses will be engaged automatically; holographic-like imagery "stamped" onto consciousness as composed of energetic *facets* tied to the "snap-shot" of an experience.

**pilot** : a professional steersman responsible for healthy functional operation of a ship toward a specific destination; in *Systemology*, an intensive trained individual qualified to specially apply *Systemology Processing* to assist other *Seekers* on the *Pathway*.

**presence** : a quality of some thing (*energy/matter*) being "present" in space-time; personal orientation of *Self* as an *Awareness* (*POV*) located in present space-time (environment) and communicating with extant energy-matter.

**processing command line (PCL)** or **command line** : a directed input; a specific command using highly selective language for *Systemology Processing*; a predetermined directive statement (cause) intended to focus concentrated attention (effect).

**processing, systematic** : the inner-workings or "through-put" result of systems; in *Systemology*, a method of applied spiritual technology used toward personal Self-Actualization; methods of selective directed attention, communicated language and associative imagery that increases personal control of the human condition.

**realization** : the clear perception of an understanding; a consideration or understanding on what is "actual"; to make "real" or give "reality" to so as to grant a property of "being-ness" or "being as it is"; the state or instance of coming to an *Awareness*; in *Systemology*, "gnosis" or true knowledge achieved during *systematic processing*; achievement of a new (or "higher") cognition, true knowledge or perception of Self; a consideration of reality or assignment of meaning.

**responsibility** : the *ability* to *respond*; the extent of mobilizing *power* and *understanding* an individual maintains as *Awareness* to enact *change*; the proactive ability to *Self-direct* and make decisions independent of an outside authority.

**Seeker** : an individual on the *Pathway to Self-Honesty*; a practitioner of *Mardukite Systemology* or *Systemology Processing*, that is working toward *Spiritual Ascension*.

**Self-actualization** : bringing the full potential of the Human spirit into Reality; expressing full capabilities and creativeness of the *Alpha-Spirit*.

**Self-determinism** : the freedom to act, clear of external control or influence; the personal control of Will to direct intention.

**Self-honesty** : the basic or original *alpha* state of *being* and *knowing*; clear and present total *Awareness* of-and-as *Self*, in its most basic and true proactive expression of itself as *Spirit* or *I-AM*—free of artificial attachments, perceptive filters and other emotionally-reactive or mentally-conditioned programming imposed on the human condition by the systematized physical world; the ability to experience existence without judgment.

**spiritual timeline** : a continuous stream of moment-to-moment *Mental Images* (or a record of experiences) that defines the "past" of a spiritual being (or *Alpha-Spirit*) and which includes impressions (*imprints, &tc.*) from all life-in-carnations and significant spiritual events the being has encountered; in Systemology, also "*backtrack.*"

**Systemology** : a modern tradition of applied religious philosophy and spiritual technology based on *Arcane Tablets* (in combination with "*general systemology*" and "*games theory*") developed in the New Age underground by Joshua Free in 2011 as an advanced futurist extension of the *Mardukite Research Org.*; also known as "*Mardukite Systemology,*" "*Metahuman Systemology*" and "*Spiritual Systemology.*"

**terminal (node)** : a point, end, or mass, on a line; a connection point for closing an electric circuit, such as a post on a battery terminating at each end of its own systematic function; a point of connectivity with other points; in systems, a contact point of interaction; a point of interaction with other points.

**turbulence** : a quality or state of distortion or disturbance that creates irregularity of a flow or pattern; the quality or state of aberration on a line (such as ragged edges) or the emotional "turbulent feelings" attached to a particular flow or terminal node; a violent, haphazard or disharmonious commotion (such as in the ebb of gusts and lulls of wind action).

**willingness** : the state of conscious Self-determined ability and interest (directed attention) to *Be*, *Do* or *Have*; a Self-determined consideration to reach, face up to (*confront*) or manage some "mass" or energy; the extent to which an individual considers themselves able to participate, act or communicate along some line, to put attention or intention on the line, or to produce (create) an effect.

*ZU* : the ancient Sumerian cuneiform sign for the archaic verb—"*to know*," "*knowingness*" or "*awareness*"; in *Mardukite Zuism and Systemology*, the active energy/matter of the "Spiritual Universe" (AN) experienced as a *Lifeforce* or *consciousness* that imbues living forms extant in the "Physical Universe" (KI); "*Spiritual Life Energy*"; energy demonstrated by the WILL of an actualized *Alpha-Spirit* in the "Spiritual Universe" (AN), which impinges its *Awareness* into the Physical Universe (KI), animating/controlling *Life* for its experience of *beta-existence* along an individual Alpha-Spirit's personal *Identity-continuum*, called a *ZU-line*.

**Zu-Line** : a theoretical construct in *Mardukite Zuism and Systemology* demonstrating *Spiritual Life Energy* (*ZU*) as a personal individual "continuum" of Awareness interacting with all Spheres of Existence on the Standard Model of

Systemology; a spectrum of potential variations and interactions of a monistic continuum or singular *Spiritual Life Energy (ZU)* demonstrated on the Standard Model; an energetic channel of potential POV and "locations" of Beingness, demonstrated in early Systemology materials as an individual Alpha-Spirit's personal *Identity-continuum*, potentially connecting *Awareness (ZU)* of *Self* with "*Infinity*" simultaneous with all points considered in existence; a symbolic demonstration of the "*Life-line*" on which *Awareness (ZU)* extends from the direction of the "Spiritual Universe" (AN) in its true original *alpha state* through an entire possible range of activity resulting in its *beta state* and control of a *genetic-entity* occupying the *Physical Universe (KI)*.

*The Systemology Professional Course*
continues in the next lesson booklet:
**HANDLING HUMANITY**

# Fundamentals of Systemology
## *in six*
## Basic Course Lesson Booklets

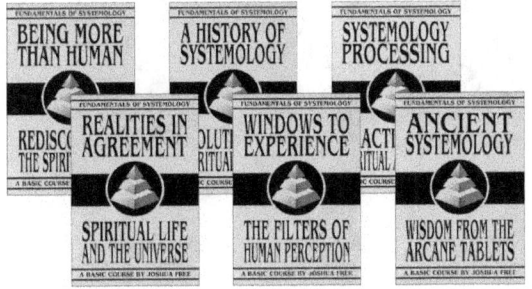

Also
available
as a
*six-in-one*
hardcover
edition!

# THE SYSTEMOL

Seekers and students of the *Basic Course* and *Professional Course* will also be interested in the *Advanced Series* of the *Systemology Core*. These volumes are a complete chronological record of the Mardukite New Thought developments from the Systemology Society, published in 2019 through 2023.

The *Systemology Core* begins with the first professional publication released when the *Mardukite Systemology Society* emerged from the underground in 2019, with: *"The Tablets of Destiny Revelation."*

# OGY PATHWAY

The Tablets of Destiny Revelation:
*How Long-Lost Anunnaki Wisdom*
*Can Change the Fate of Humanity*

Crystal Clear: *Handbook for Seekers*

Metahuman Destinations (2 *volumes*)

Imaginomicon:
*Approaching Gateways to Higher Universes*

Way of the Wizard: *Utilitarian Systemology*

Systemology-180: *Fast-Track to Ascension*

Systemology Backtrack:
*Reclaiming Spiritual Power & Past-Life Memory*

PUBLISHED BY THE **JOSHUA FREE** IMPRINT REPRESENTING

**The Mardukite Academy of Systemology**

**mardukite.com**

www.ingramcontent.com/pod-product-compliance
Lightning Source LLC
Chambersburg PA
CBHW071215120626
46546CB00006B/2569